Build A Room

A Collection Of Poems, Prose, Essays, And Flash Fiction

Jeff Lightly

FejjMo Publishing, LLC

To all those who write.

The struggle is real but you can persevere — believe in YOU!

To write is to think – William Faulkner

Contents

Introduction

Thank you for spending part of your time reading this offering, the contents vary in style and genre but often reflect my personal feelings about the subject matter. Then again, sometimes I just flat out made things up! Such is the beauty of writing.

I have included poems, prose, essays, and flash fiction that I have written throughout the years.

The poems, often written through a stream-of-consciousness approach, are meant to provoke thought beyond the words. I urge you to consider those words and interpret them in your own, personal way. You may never understand my motivations and it is not required. If you can take a thought, idea, or a motivation away from the words, then I have done my job.

Some of the writings reflect actual events in my life; Drifter's Homecoming reflects on my addiction recovery, Am I Bukowski? lays out my struggles as a writer as I question myself and my abilities. Others were simply born from the imagination; JoyRide is one. Another one, Lazy Daisy is a stream-of-consciousness piece that popped into my head and was written in fifteen minutes — sometimes it happens that way. I'm still not sure where I picked up this storyline but I followed it, hopefully to your enjoyment. Other times, it takes years, as in the case of Three Bullets. I spent over two years writing and rewriting, trying to make my first effort as polished as possible. An excerpt of this, my first novel, is included.

Good, Night

Days need, days bleed, days seed.

I dream them, night needs them.

Sun helps make the days but clouds get in the way...then what?

It's still the day

        until it's night.

Night, that time of fright,

of loves delight.

Party time, yeah, dark time,

        uh-huh.

Can it stay day,

keep night away

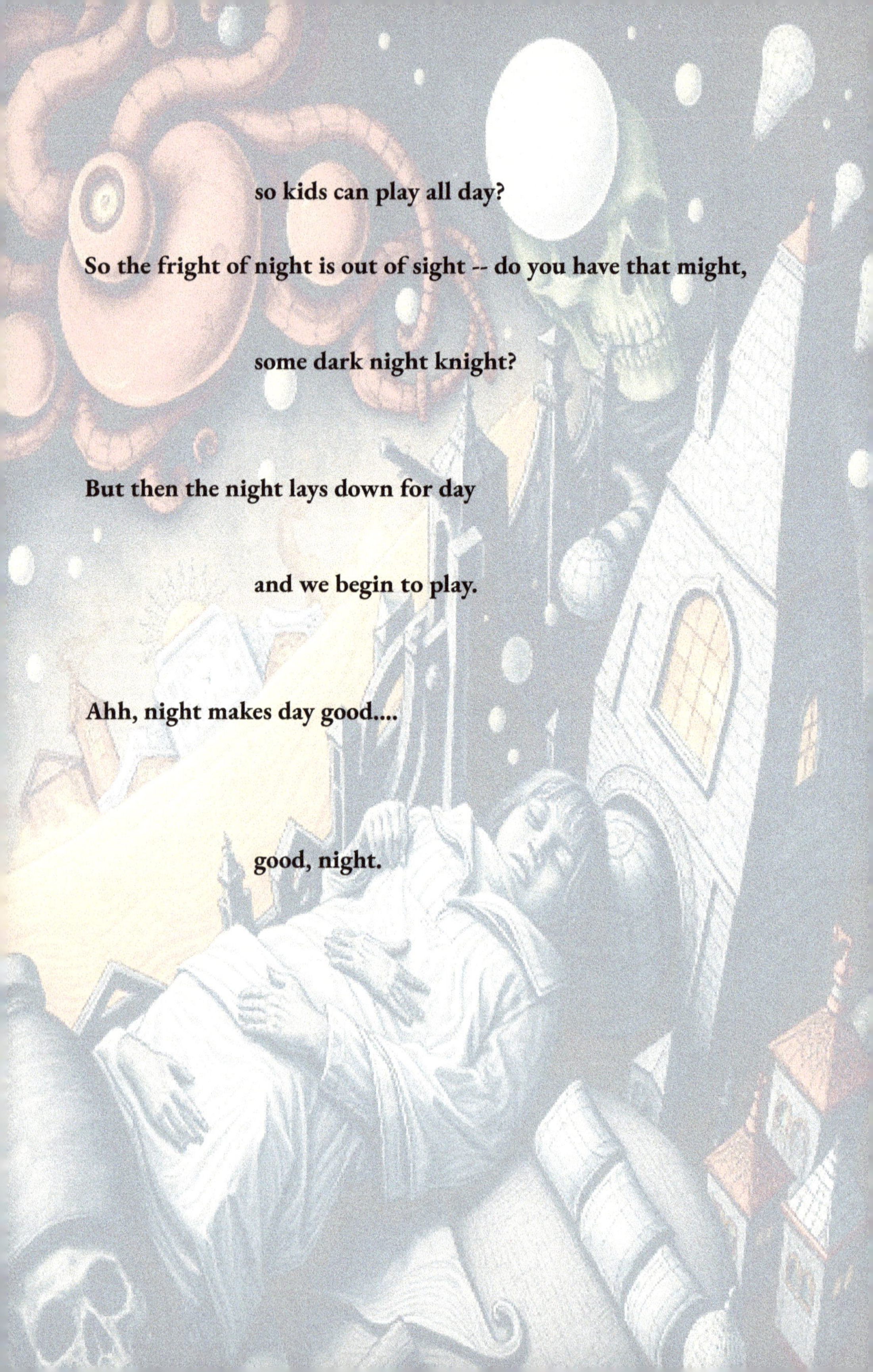

so kids can play all day?

So the fright of night is out of sight -- do you have that might,

some dark night knight?

But then the night lays down for day

and we begin to play.

Ahh, night makes day good....

good, night.

RobGod

Banging, clanging, bells will be chirping,

criminals be perping.

The church, to the church!
They stole from the church as the bells pealed,

they peeled off hundreds from the
offering,

proffering.

Their black masks to the children, leave them be, kids.

A car *screeeeeeches* away...

Drifter's Homecoming

Once a drifter, now flying through the clouds.

Blackness once pervasive, chased by the brilliant, white sunlight.

Crouched low for years, now standing tall.

Quiet, almost invisible in the darkness.

Now speaking out loud to a freshly awakened soul.

Desperate cries became a stepping-stone

.   into

.   life's

.   newly

.   made

.   staircase.

{you can see forever up here}

Past weeds are ripped up, revealing ugly, twisted, and tormented roots.

They lay dead on the ground,

Rotting.

In the freshly disturbed soil seeds sprout.

A TREE, the strong and resourceful oak.

GRASS, giving freshness and comfort underfoot.

They both sway in the breeze, playfully.

A FLOWER, encouraging nature to gather;

beauty for all to see.

{hush}

The drifter sits against the oak,

feels the soft grass.

The flower's aroma surrounds him...

He has finally come home.

Am I Bukowski?

River don't dance and the romance is a no-showmance.

Life and the way it

Gets-in-its-way

leaves me with   nothing to say.

Sometimes.

Other times,

I can't shut up   or step up   or get up.

Am I like Bukowski?

Dream it, bitch, dream it.

Lay down,

          stay down,

          pray.

Down.

I stay down,

bring you down, down.

Wrong answer, amigo!

Bootstraps - grab 'em and get.

Get far from here   and   far from   me.

So far that when you turn back to me, it's me you cannot see.

More steps and I never was, you see.

So buzz away, for your own good, as you should.

Be a bee.

Am I Bukowski?

Closer but days away. That power is not out yet. Maybe it lurks,

maybe it <hides>

and rides and rides and rides.

But know ... no.

Glad you left, for you I'm glad,

for me

I'm sad   and mad   and lost.

But I'm no Bukowski, am I?

I can't care about that yet,

                or ever.

For sure,

            never.

Will the river dance again?

Is there enough water

to hip and to hop

or

two-step it when it flows in Texas?

This is the nexus, perhaps.

I want to be Bukowski,   but alive.

Fuckers.

Solution

I BE FLOATSY, BACKWARDS toesy.

Pop pop pop.

That ain't my mind, it the sound of sorrow from yesterday, today,
tomorrow.

Speak up yo!

You the problem

        in a bottle, aint no Genie,

add something to it,

        some kind of solution,

get   absolution.
Resolve, absolve.

Rise.

Above.

Above you can see it can't you?

Well, can't you?

[yes].

Do it son, go!

Lazy Daisy

Lookie here she be hay-zee.

Her man's a zero,

                ain't no hero,

jumpin' round all day, fire in his feet

                boiled up the hate
                in his heart.

Stay in the far away place when he roils around, Daisy or not. And
keep your eye offa   her,

                you ain't gettin' off with her even
                though she ain't choosy

she like you - is like you, wanna be more like you.

Weren't for Mr Hot Foot, she'd cozy up with you,

do what you want to do,

show you a trick or two too.

Someday maybe her head clear up

           and she'll come clear up.

To you.

But your outlook is hazy, not unlike Daisy.

Later in the summer

You got that shiver, Daisy's man up the river and she comes walkin'
and talkin, hot   footin' your way.

Oh what to say or,

stay away?

Mr Hot Foot,

        what's his reach yet?

        who has he met yet?

Are you scared yet?

Daisy is closer and you see the dukes, that's right.

She has that way,

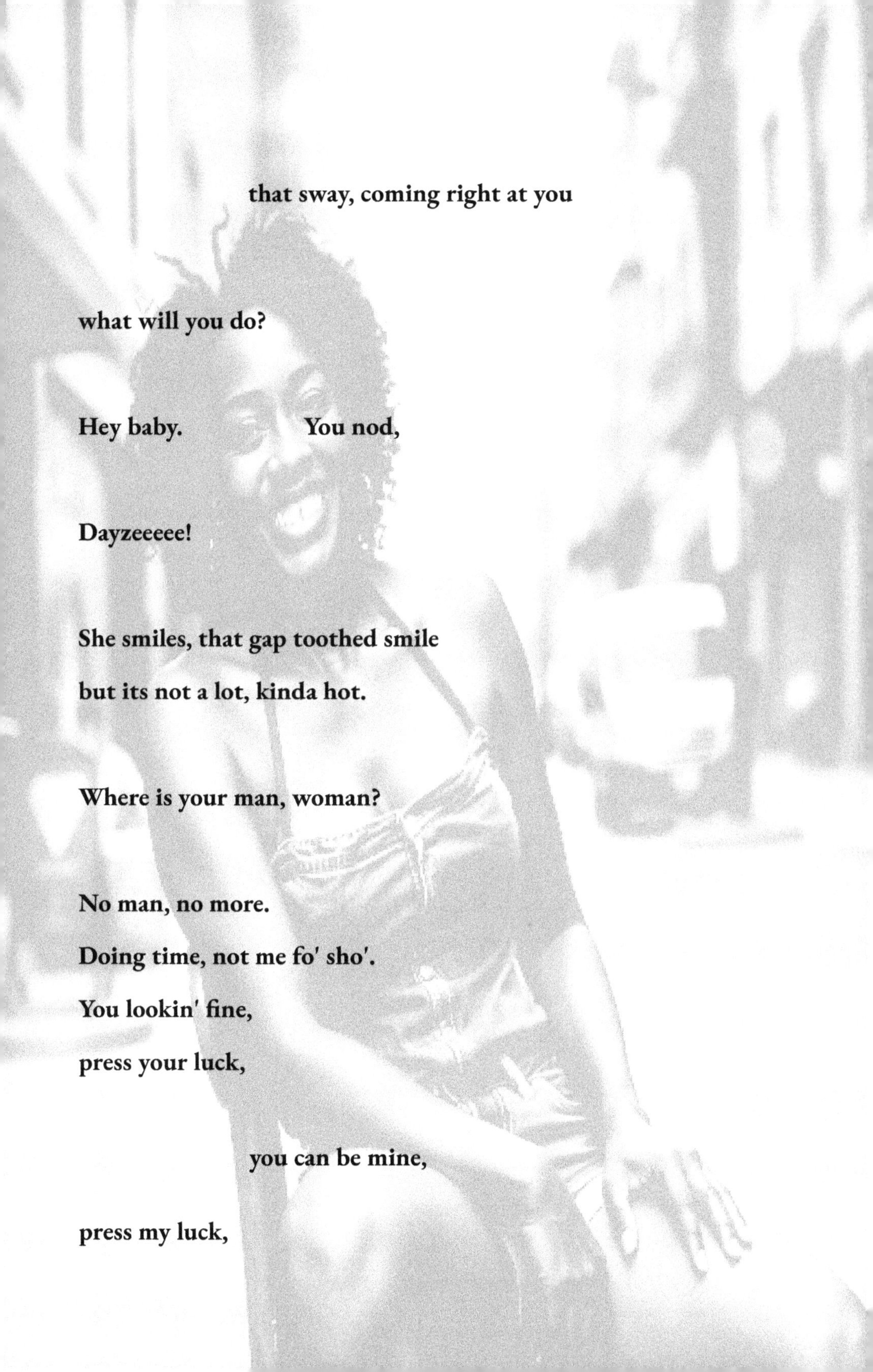

     that sway, coming right at you

what will you do?

Hey baby.   You nod,

Dayzeeeee!

She smiles, that gap toothed smile
but its not a lot, kinda hot.

Where is your man, woman?

No man, no more.
Doing time, not me fo' sho'.
You lookin' fine,
press your luck,

    you can be mine,

press my luck,

you WILL be mine.

I know you watch me, I ain't blind.

I'll be around.

Watch me walk away, OK?

It's OK,

for you I'd sway.

Cheeks flush, aw, Daisy, that's crazy, your man do me damage I look at you that way.

No man, no more. Watch me go. Or not ... bet you do.

Of course he does.

Next day Daisy sits outside,

hot outside,

she's hot outside.

The sidewalk shimmers the summer, she sweats — evenly.

Wooden chair cradling her ass,   legs slightly spread.

She sees you coming.

Gap-tooth spreads her lips in a pleasant smile,

eases his mind,

teases his mind,

pleases his mind,

no he don't mind.

He gets nearer, she sits up, then back again,

stretching her back

                but her back is fine.

She arches for you,

                McDonald's arches for you,

                Gateway Arches for you.

It's for you but are you seein' it   and believin' it?

Whatchu gonna do about it?

The boy shy,

years away from getting high,

she's grabbing for his youth,

bending that around in her mind.

A drop of sweat rolls between her breasts

and she knows it,

feels the flow of it,
doesn't let go of it.
He sees that and he's mine

she thinks,

he does and   he thinks

and thinks   and thinks.

There you are baby boy, I've been waiting for you,

just for you,

only you.

Now tell me, whatchu gonna do?

His breath escapes in a mad rush.

Don't be shy baby boy, Daisy is here for you,

near for you,

she may even do anything for you.

Now its his turn to sweat. Breathless and unsure, hot flashing cheeks.

He sees her up close now,

those lips

and those clothes

and her   soft   colored   legs.

He'd love to feel them but he doesn't dare,

so he'll just stare til she takes his hand.

I said don't be shy baby boy.

I'll take care of you,

play truth or dare with you,

do what you wanna do.

I know you want it too.

I can see it with my eyes,   the one thing a man can't hide.

She licks her lips and looks up at him

— gap —

that sexy sweet gap.

He turns and runs, afraid,

excited,

ignited!

You'll be back baby boy.

The gap disappears.

Daisy, girl be crazy — thinks everyone maybe —

but they don't really know.

She wants love,

needs love,

will give love;

not just that sex stuff,   no.

She wants a man to care for,

to be for,

to get home for,

to go to work for,

to show off to mom,

to feel happy and wanted.

Not sad and lonely.

The boy seems nice,

she wants to entice,

she sure can entice now can't she?

The other men see her too but they just think of the one.

Thing, one thing only   but they be lonely too,

they just don't care yet.

Daisy cares now,

wants the boy now

          and not just his manhood but his
          "be good".

She thinks of him and sees them at a movie.

She thinks of him and

          reaches between her legs,
          for sure.

She thinks of him eating a home cooked meal,   made by her,   for
him,   for them

and it makes her feel good inside.

Even better than the feeling of a man inside.

She wants the package,

        the love

        the whole, the whole damn thing.

And why not, man?

Why not?

Another bead of sweat rolls between her breasts

        but she doesn't notice —

daydreams of The Whole Thing get in the way.

Other men on the street notice   but she don't notice them.

She's too busy watching

the boy

        walk down the street,

in her mind.

JoyRide

The pavement sings and rings as they *swooshed* and rolled on down

the road.

Where to go? They don't know, Joe...or Jo?

Windows down wind does blasting, crank that radio motherfucker, that's Jimi! Singing Mary!

Water ring, hula dancer, dusty dash, don't seem to matter.

Move along, groove along. You get tired, just say so long.

Drifter, drifting, drifted, drifts...spinning my head. What's in this weed?

some   thing wrong.

Driver!   Driver......he sags.

From a distance,

the crash is dusty and quiet,

up close,

devastating.

Raft In A Garage

I'VE GOT A RAFT full of dust.

Up in the rafters, of course.

Never been in the water, never sailed anywhere.

I could pull that raft

down

(If I'd only try)

and wash it off, take it to the river (Take Me To The River), and talk your head off.

Take it to the lake and get drifty.

Take it to the gulf and run into an oil well.

Take it to the ocean and I won't be seen anymore.

It's a risk man, and a damn shame too.

Waste of raft the way it sits,

      waste of life not using it.

I don't sit in the rafters but I might as well...

      Life's dust,

it stings,

yeah,

      like hell.

I could risk it all and go on that journey or trip or adventure or voyage.

Become a seafaring man.

I'm too afraid.

And the dust

Keeps

MOUNTING.

Sewer Rat Instructions

17 AND I LOVED her. She laughed at my jokes, we got each other, Mommy and Daddy rich, mine, nah. She didn't care but that mutha sure did. Young love, puppy love for sure. There goes my heart, there goes my virginity. Scared. Friend advises "You gotta break up with her, don't be tied down" I did, Idiot! Regrets linger, cuz, who knows? OK, teen love almost never is what it seems but man, what if? The funniest, shittiest, saddest part is this; the nickname of the friend who gave me that crap advise? *Sewer Rat!* What was wrong with me? We'll never know how her and I would have danced in life. The what if hurts on this one.

I whisper her name...

Gonna Dig Me A Hole

I HAVE THE SPADE ready to go, it's just waiting for me to jump up a bit in the air and then down on it and get to digging. It hasn't been used yet, so the sun occasionally glints off the business end of the shovel and into wherever light goes when no one can see it. The shovel's shaft is clean and smooth with a light oak varnish. It's a pretty one right now but just you wait shovel, that varnish will get worn down, the sun isn't going to dance off of you much longer, not when I get done here today, no sir! I've got a hole to dig and I plan on doing it until the sun goes down and maybe even later if there is moonlight. No, that moon won't be able to shoot its light down from up there and hit my shovel and go running off into god knows where moonlight goes where no one can see it. I wonder if it goes to the same place as the sunlight. I bet it does. All the work I'm going to do is going to scuff off the shine of this here new shovel like nobody's business, mark my word. I just hope I don't wear this shovel out by the end of the day, all the digging I've got to do. Come to think of it, I'd have to ask my daddy for more money to buy another shovel when this one gets worn down later. You see, I spent the last of my allowance plus the twelve dollars and a quarter I had saved up in the back of my sock drawer. I keep my money there, figuring that nobody wants to root around in another guy's socks. Even though they are clean, momma sees to that, she takes care of everything like that around the house. Her and daddy get along real good, always smiling at each other. In fact, they were smiling at each other a lot when daddy says to me to run along with my new shovel and go up a piece and over the hill and start digging. I asked him what you want me to dig daddy? And he said to dig a hole, he said dig it in a big old circle in that field down the hill. Make it really wide at first and once you have the grass dug up and the circle is big enough, start digging deeper. I don't know what he has planned, but I'm sure going to dig one big hole for him. I wonder if he wants to put in a swimming pool. I've seen pictures where some pools are round and he wants a round hole. I bet it is a swimming pool! Man, that will be so nice on a hot day like today, jump in the water and splash mom and daddy. Maybe have some friends over and splash them too. I bet all the kids in the county are going to want to come over to my swimming pool and splash. Gosh, this is going to be fun! I sure like this idea better than the one daddy came up with the last time him and momma smiled at each other a bunch. He wanted me to mow the pasture but I said no daddy, what will the cows eat if I do that? And he says, set the dang mower up higher and they can eat just fine and the pasture will look real good and all the neighbors will know we take pride in our farm. The mower is an old one but it runs just fine. It's not shiny at all so don't you expect any sun to go whooshing off of it anytime soon. And never you mind about the moonlight, it's not a good idea to be mowing in the dark, no sir, do not do that, ok? I ought to paint it silver so it does make that light go soaring. I'll ask daddy about that because I'll need for him to get me some paint on account of I spent all my money on this here shovel. Well, I have to get to digging, like they say, the hole ain't gonna dig itself. Who would say such a thing? Of course, it ain't gonna dig itself, everybody knows that. People say some funny things now and again! Whew, it is starting to get hot out here already and it's not quite noon. I think I'll scurry up that little rise over there and sit in the shade for a spell, get my strength saved up. Besides, I'll be able to get a good look at the land where I'm going to dig that big ol' hole. Planning is what that is and that little hill will be a good spot to do that. This is going to be some pool! Now, I just had me a thought about digging this hole; what in the world am I supposed to do with all the dirt I get? Maybe I ought to be asking daddy about that before I even start. My luck, I'd pile up the dirt into a big old hill and he won't want that. Then what? I don't mind working, I'm a good worker, daddy says, but I heard a fella say that you ought to work smarter, not harder. Now, I didn't quite get that at first, but I was just about to drift off to sleep one night and I'll be danged if it didn't hit me like a ton of bricks! It's like you should do some thinking about what you're doing. I gotta think about this before I even start digging. Being smarter is what that is! Daddy says I am the smartest of all his kids, at least the boys. And he says don't go telling people that so, do me a favor, and don't tell nobody, deal?

Well, I'll be if I don't hear momma calling me in for lunch. She must be done smiling at daddy. I'll have to ask daddy if he really wants me to dig this hole. I suppose if he does, I'll have to come back after I eat and get it started. Be a shame to scuff up this shovel. It is brand new, after all.

I should get back home. I'm hungry and I didn't want to dig no hole anyways.

When I Was Young

Previously published in Flash Frontier Magazine, March 2023

When I was young, the days seemed longer, summer was muggier, winter colder. Everything seemed so far off and we couldn't wait to turn thirteen, eighteen, twenty-one. People over thirty really were old it seemed.

I'd watch Walter Cronkite rattle off last week's Vietnam casualty count, a perverse Death Scoreboard; Viet Cong: 289 dead, U.S: 74 dead. My reaction, "YES, we won!", not unlike my reaction when the Vikings won a football game.

When I was young, I usually was told what to do, at least for any decision above, though not always, what shoes to wear. I had to go to school, to church, to grandma's. I'd protest to deaf ears.

I'm no longer young but the days can still seem long, summer certainly is muggier, and I'm tired of the cold weather. I wish I was thirteen again (sort of), or eighteen again (yes), or twenty-one again (definitely). Thirty is young.

Walter is gone and I reconciled my youthful ignorance about war.
It is nothing to celebrate, not "our" team's side or "theirs". They all
had families who ached then and now.

I get to make most decisions in life. I like that. I enjoy taking online
classes to keep learning. I'm at peace with my spirituality.

I miss grandma.

Trestle Walk

The engineer scowled at us as the train sailed past, easily going fifty and causing our hair to swirl around in a mad, frantic dance. As the train receded from view, my hair fluttered slower and slower, then drifted back down on my head in a messy bunch. But that didn't matter now.

"You going to run across the trestle? Or are you still chicken?" asked Mitch. The other boys laughed nervously.

Sure didn't care about the way he talked to me. The tracks didn't scare me, but what was the point? No more than walking on the street. You just need to navigate over the dark brown and oily-smelling ties. Unless a train came. Today I was going to do it and show others my fearlessness, leading the way and becoming a hero in their eyes. On their deathbeds, they would remember this day and remember me!

I took a deep breath to quell my excitement. My journey began with small steps up the rock-covered incline, then over the first rail. I turned down the tracks, staring into the sun. The trestle bridge loomed before me, peeling paint on its powerful angled iron entrance, daring me to come forward.

With more steps toward my destiny, dust kicked up and hung in the still summer air. Arriving at the bridge, I turned to look at my friends in the distance. None of them moved, but all of them watched me. My eyes focused on the rows of giant rivets somehow still holding the structure upright. Rust stains fell from each rivet, creating orange-red tears that took years to fall. I wanted to reach out and touch one, maybe wipe a tear away, but the rush of the river thirty feet below diverted my attention.

Another deep breath and more steps forward, taking care to land on the center of each tie. The wood was old, but I could feel its strength beneath my dirty, worn tennis shoes. I thought about the trees that created them, wondering where they grew and when they were harvested. If only they could talk. This proved to be a distraction. On the next step, my focus was gone, and I missed the center of the tie, turning my ankle slightly. I stumbled a bit but was able to catch my fall with my hand on a rail. An instant vision of being trapped between two ties, legs dangling beneath the bridge as a train approached. The summer sun made the rail hot, and the discomfort brought me back to reality. A sharp pain ran up the outside of my ankle but was gone as soon as it came.

My breathing became rapid. Was that a train whistle? One step followed another. And another. And another. Halfway across now. My friends were yelling something, but I didn't dare turn and look their way, fearing I would lose my balance again. My pace picked up even more. All of my focus was on the ties and my feet. I was almost there! The brown water gurgled below. Don't look down, I reminded myself. Five more ties and the journey will be complete. Four more, three more. I jumped past the remaining ties and was on the other side. Arms raised straight in the air, victorious! I did it! I turned and yelled at my friends, "Now who's the chicken?"

But they were gone. I was the sole witness to this feat. My arms dropped to my side.

"You fuckers!", I shouted across the bridge and began to laugh. With a deep breath, I retraced my journey back across the bridge, smiling all the way.

Witness

We both knew he was going to suffer; what he had done was far too serious to escape punishment.

"He's home. Quick, hide in the closet," he ordered. Without thought, I complied and crouched down as he shut the sliding doors. We both giggled a nervous laugh.

Murmurs from the other room. Shouting. Footsteps heading our way. The bedroom door flies open. Dad shouting — louder and louder. Brother trying and failing to explain. Peering through the crack in the door, my eyes widen as it begins.

An eternity later, it was over.

Why I hid in the closet still baffles and haunts me fifty years later.

Six Word Flash Fiction

Her headphones blocked out the world.

Books wanted but words are scarce.

He was dead. He was unaware.

Searing summer sun-bronzed beach bodies bake.

Trampled flowers can grow back beautifully.

Careful! Careful! The way is icy.

The baby smiles and worries fade.

My math skills? Horrible. (Insert laughter.)

Look forward, wear shades if needed.

He looked ahead. No shades required.

Mediocrity is borne from 'good enough'.

Her salty tears made him walk.

She smiled with her eyes, slowly.

Realizing she needs hospice crushes me.

Rain falls, bees swarm, flowers...pretty.

Untitled Because I Don't Know What To Think Anymore

WHEN I ENTERED MY apartment, I threw that damn jacket on the couch and paced the floor. Looking around the room, it was obvious that I'd been slacking off again but can you blame me? OK, this room is a mess, over there in the kitchen there are dishes piled up, and when was the last time this carpet got vacuumed? I really can't remember and I just don't care. It had been a busy, fucked up time and playing housekeeper just wasn't in the cards. Besides, I don't have people over much, hardly ever actually. That jacket slid off the couch with a slow, soft, sliding sound and crumpled in a pile. I watched it fall and just stood there not making any attempt to catch it. When events like tonight's fun-and-games happen, I just get frustrated. I mean, I was so close, so fucking close! Rather, I thought I was.

I thought the party was going well, I even got up and sang karaoke! I was feeling sky high and was really glad my buddy invited me over. He knew she'd be there. He knew I didn't know that. Thought it'd be a nice surprise. More important, he knew how I was crushing on her. Whenever I'd see her, at work or like tonight, at the party, I would literally get weak-kneed. Seriously, I felt my knees sag tonight when she walked in the room. I had to wonder if she heard me singing. I can't say if I hoped so or hoped not.

I don't know what I was thinking but I slid over next to the snack table, near her. I could hear her sweet, sweet voice. I swear I could smell her too. Well, that so-called sweet, sweet voice let her friend know that the guy who was just singing has been creeping around work and she should probably leave. Her friend had heard the karaoke guy wanted to do more than creep around her, if you know what I mean.

So she just laughed and told her friend that the creep had the weirdest jacket she'd ever seen.

That's when I scooped up that so-called weird jacket and came home, where I'm at right now. Music helps me calm down so I just put my earbuds in, hit shuffle on my playlist.

I love Beck's music. The dude is so creative.

First song shuffled up?

Loser.

Sums up the night I'd say.

That jacket can just stay on the floor.

A Eulogy

CARRYING ON WITHOUT OUR loved ones can be difficult, but that very act of carrying on will honor them.

Let's honor those we have lost.

Today, as we honor the memory of my brother, Rick, I also want to honor those of you here. I know you have grieved the loss of Rick and also for losing many other friends and family we miss yet today. I'd like to read portions from two Psalms and offer my thoughts.

Psalm 6, verse 6 says:

6 I am worn out from my groaning.

All night long I flood my bed with weeping

and drench my couch with tears.

Many of us can relate to that passage. The tears we have shed are many and the aches we often feel for our loss are deep. It can take a toll on our bodies and leave us tired and weary.

I ask you to shed those tears and experience the loss but, when you are ready, dry those tears, rest your body and your soul, and come back to your friends and family. We are here for each other.

...and Psalm 55, verses 4 through 8 says:

4 My heart is in anguish within me;

the terrors of death have fallen on me.

5 Fear and trembling have beset me;

horror has overwhelmed me.

6 I said, "Oh, that I had the wings of a dove!

I would fly away and be at rest.

7 I would flee far away

and stay in the desert;

8 I would hurry to my place of shelter,

Far from the tempest and storm."

The death of a loved one can be frightening, not knowing what our future will be without them.

No doubt many have felt the urge to fly far, far away because the tempest that death can create overwhelms us.

Feel those feelings - you need to!

Fly away to your place of shelter and seek that comfort if you must - but please come back to us. We need each other.

Let's honor those we have lost.

Carrying on without our loved ones can be difficult, but that very act of carrying on will honor them.

Lessons In Dying - An Essay

HE LAY THERE ON his side, trapped in a nursing home. Trapped in a body missing a leg. Trapped in a mind scalded by strokes.

He grimaced as he reached his hand into the backside of his pajamas. I wasn't sure what he was doing but I was certain he was in a great deal of discomfort. He brought his hand out from under his clothing and waved it across the wall next to his bed. A semicircle of feces appeared, dark brown against the pale green paint. I sat there frozen for a moment, unsure how to react to this. Seeing someone smear their own shit against a wall is not something I see regularly. I didn't have the cleaning supplies, the gloves, and, most importantly, the stomach to clean this mess up. I went to the nurses station and let them know what was going on. "Oh, he must be constipated again.", was the nurses response. "I'll be right down." And she did. I was told he had done this before and they suspected he was constipated and this was, in his mind, the way to solve the dilemma.

In the year and a half before he died, this man, my grandfather, had lost so much. His wife died unexpectedly at home. She had been his caregiver in addition to his wife of fifty plus years. Someone else had to take on that role. This was too big of a job for family. A care facility search was started. They had a dog that had to be re-homed. One month later he had a stroke that all but ended his conversational ability; more on that later. That's a great deal of trauma in such a short time and must have been agonizing for this 89 year-old man.

I've had several people wonder why he was being tested, why these bad things were happening to him. Was this karma come calling? Though he wasn't a saint he also was not a bad man by any stretch. Certainly not to be punished by the universe this way. If nature was going to equitably even the score he'd have deserved a leaky roof two years in a row, not this wicked physical injury.

The focus seemed to be on the person going through the slow march towards death when I counter with another theory. What if this whole dying process was for us, those of us watching the decline towards the inevitable? After all, my grandfather's time was short - that was obvious to all. Why would the universe then try to teach him a lesson? I'd sooner think his mind was reminiscing about his life, not studying the lesson at hand. There's not much of a need to learn more at that juncture in life. No, we were the ones in the lecture hall being schooled not on death, but on life. We still had the time and the need to learn. To be reminded of the cliché but true idiom, 'live each day as if it were your last'. But if one pays attention, there is more. It can show you that some things that happen towards the end of life can be embarrassing if not full on humiliating to the sufferer as well as the survivor. And once you see that you might learn how to comfort your loved one, assuring them that it's ok this embarrassment happened, that it can be handled properly. You can learn the compassion and grace that the dying needs. You can, if you really pay attention, learn about the dying process and all its stages so that the next time, you'll be even better prepared to help the dying. Perhaps then, too, when the time becomes yours, you may know and be comforted by the knowledge of what lay ahead. And if through your journey your friends and family have observed your grace and your willingness to learn about such a difficult and personal event, they will show you the compassion, the grace, that you learned, that you too deserve.

Once we learn that giving of yourself to those in need is important, these acts of caring can be applied in our lives everyday and to everyone, giving credence and clarity to that cliché.

Live each day as if it were your last. Not only because it might be cliché but because living that way can help us all live happier and more meaningful lives.

Book Excerpt - Wandering And The Light It Sheds

THAT LAST BREATH LEFT with a slow, soft sigh. So soft that Ethan did not realize that was his wife's final breath. Holding her hand and bent over at the waist, he looked at her and half-smiled — thinking that he could charm her to stay in this world. She remained still, as she had for the past few weeks. Peaceful and still as he talked to her throughout each day. Each day another slow but wonderful walk through their lives together. Reminding her of what they had. Inferring, he hoped, that she should stick around for more memories. Like California! She loved the beach and the Pacific. She once said to him, "Ethan, I wish I could look towards an island somewhere out in the vastness. And knowing just where it is, snap my fingers and we're there. I would do that all day if I could! You'd go with me, wouldn't you?" Of course he would.

He held that pose and that smile even as the heart monitor changed tunes from an erratic beep, pause, beep, pause song to a new, solo tune that comprised one long, single note. Such a sad song; he cried. He smiled still as the nurse came in, followed by a doctor half Ethan's age. More than once did he think this doctor would be about their son's age, had he lived. But he didn't. Ethan Jr. died two days after he was born — in this very hospital — two floors down. He died without ever tossing Ethan the elder a baseball or causing him grief by crashing the family car.

He touched her left arm, bruised from the IV lines hooked into her veins; the cardiac telemetry box, with its wires octopussing their way over her upper body, connecting to metal snaps stuck to her skin. The thin tube looped around her ears with the oxygen tips placed just below her nose.

"Mr. Turner," began the nurse, "I'm afraid she's gone. Mr. Turner?"

The half-smile remained, but Ethan could feel his life changing.

With a quick flick of his finger, the doctor silenced the heart monitor as a DJ would shut off his mixer for the night. It left the room with that still and empty white noise; that silence that is, in reality, so very loud. That silent hum took the smile from Ethan's face. He wondered if it would ever come back.

For an instant he concluded that she was going to be fine, some technical glitch with the machine. Doc is just rebooting the thing. It's a machine, after all; machines break all the time, right? Relieved, he sat down next to Elise, his wife of nearly forty years.

"You scared me! Wow, please don't do that again!" he said as he brushed her brown but graying hair.

"Mr. Turner? Mr. Turner, your wife is gone. I am so sorry," said the young doctor.

"No, son, mom is fine. She'll be talking in a minute or two," said Ethan, blending lost hopes and dreams with this moment.

The nurse looked at the doctor, brow furrowed with sad overtones The doctor was all business today. "Time of death, 2:32 p.m."

The good doctor's pager chose that time to beep-beep-beep awake, much to the good doctor's relief as he left the room to do more good doctoring and also leaving the follow-up tasks for the nurse.

"Mr. Turner, please sit next to Elise." The nurse scooted a small chair in behind Ethan, making gentle skidding sounds as it went across the faux wood floor.

"Thank you. Where is the doctor going? For more help?" Ethan sat, never taking his eyes from Elise. Maybe she just needs some sleep, he thought and then said, "Would some sleep help her any? Maybe we could dim the lights a bit for her." His lip quivered.

"The doctor has done everything possible for your wife and he is needed elsewhere. I can tell you loved her very much. It seems you've been at the hospital more than I have in the past month. Stay with her as long you want. We're in no hurry here."

Ethan stood up and turned towards the window; his back turned to the two women. From that vantage point, he watched the soft, white clouds float by in the distance. At that instant, he wondered if Elise was caught up in the one particularly white, soft cloud.

"She's always been daring so I'm not going to be surprised if she is flying with that cloud. You see the one I'm talking about?"

"Mr. Turner?"

"That cloud … it has … Elise. Wait, no."

Ethan craned his neck to the right, taking in the last vision of the cloud. He returned to his chair and gazed at his wife.

"She's gone. She's gone, isn't she?" he asked.

"I'm sorry Mr. Turner but she is. Can I call someone for you? Anyone?" asked the nurse. She leaned against the bed rail, across from Ethan, and reached her hand out.

He took her gloved hand and thought how odd it must be to wear nitrile gloves all day; taking them off, putting them on; all day, every day; did it leave her hands smelling like whatever nitrile is?

"We have no family. I'll call … somebody. What do I do now?"

"Mr. Turner, stay here for awhile, talk to her if you need to. I'll be back with staff later and, when you are ready, we can clean the room up and take care of your wife. Would that be OK?"

Ethan waved her off, at least, weeks later, he thought he did. Whether he did or did not wave her away, she left.

Alone with his thoughts, Ethan sat next to Elise, quiet and calm. His world was Elise and now that world was gone; at least changed. He felt silent. No, silenced. At a slow and deliberate pace, the hospital noises began to creep into the room; a public address calling for Dr. So-and-So, code blue, room garbled. Beeps and wails mashed in with laughter and what's-for-lunches. Housekeeping wants to clean. Come on in.

Ethan wished the quiet would have stayed. Of course, it wouldn't, couldn't.

For the first time in weeks, Ethan cried. He cried when he kissed the lifeless body of Elise — he noticed she was getting cold and considered covering her in another blanket but caught himself and the irrationality of that action. He cried, standing in front of the hospital elevator; would the car ever arrive? A young couple stood next to him as he sobbed, bobbing shoulders and muffled sniffling. The pair had not lived long enough to know what to do, so they ignored Ethan. When the three of them entered the elevator car, Ethan was wiping his eyes. The young couple wondered out loud what they were going to do for supper.

"Fried chicken. Make some fried chicken when you get home. Elise, that's my wife … was my wife … is still really. Anyway, her secret ingredient was a generous dose of cinnamon in the flour. Give it a try," offered Ethan.

"Ew, yeah, we don't cook very much," replied the girl. She eyed her young husband with that help-get-me-out-of-this look, which he didn't pick up on.

"Just a thought," said Ethan. His mouth watered for that fried chicken. "I think I'll make some tonight."

Ethan turned and smiled at the pair, but the elevator came to a halt. The door opened, and the couple hurried out before they needed to respond. Ethan didn't notice; he was thinking about fried chicken.

The soft, white clouds that may or may not have carried Elise away, gave way to their alter ego — heavy, dark clouds shedding rain; it was dotting thin dribs and drabs along the blacktop. The air smelled fresh and pure; the wonderful scent only created by a soft rain. Ethan stood on the crosswalk and looked up to the room where he knew Elise lay. The curtains were now closed, which gave him pause, gave him sadness. It was as if a chapter of a book ended or, perhaps the book itself. The rain gave cover to his tears. He leaned back just a bit, then a bit more. He wanted to feel the rain splash on his face.

"Hey man, get the fuck out of the road," came the horn-accompanied shout from a cab driver, making his way to the emergency room entrance.

Without comment, Ethan moved on. A gasping, screaming very pregnant woman in the back seat of the cab ignored Ethan as they drove by.

He had arrived at the hospital shortly after four that morning, blessing him with the first row parking spot. "Rock star!" was how he would announce his premium parking location. He always said that, said it out loud even, and he was always alone. The stellar spot only afforded him respite from the rain, which he didn't care about — no, didn't even think about.

He didn't think about how Elise had gone with him to the Mercedes dealer to pick out this car; a present to himself for an early retirement. She was still well enough to get out and about and generally take care of herself, though there were obvious signs of her illness, ALS. She had been diagnosed with this disease two years prior to her death. This prompted Ethan to move up his retirement plans. He knew he would have to be her caretaker but, more important to him, he wanted — needed — to spend as much time with her as possible. He was able to sell his share in his company, VisionPlan, to his partner, Kent. Those two started the financial planning firm just two years out of college; both men not wanting to follow orders but to be leaders. That decision led to financially comfortable lives for them and their families. One day he would be pleased with that decision, just not today.

Numb, he didn't think about getting in the car and driving home. He just found himself sitting in the driveway, staring at the side of his home. His empty home. The thought kept him frozen in place, hands in lap, seatbelt still on, car still running.

His neighbors to the west, Reg and Lonni, were tending to their flower beds under their front windows when they saw Ethan pull in.

"Reg, Ethan is back and he's just sitting there. You don't suppose … ?" Lonni's question trailed off.

"Maybe. Let's give him a minute. If she did pass today he may need to be by himself for a bit."

"Oh, we can't just let him suffer alone. Come on Reg, let's go over there," said Lonnie.

They both stood up, brushed the dirt from their knees and walked toward Ethan, removing their gardening gloves along the way.

Ethan's vision was now doubled and obscured by the welling tears as he contemplated going inside. By himself. Again.

"Ethan? Ethan honey!" said Lonni.

Startled, Ethan swung his head to the left, the tears falling from his eyes and splashing his cheek and arm. He reached for the window control but accidentally hit the passenger side window button, then the door lock, and finally, the driver's window was sliding down.

"Oh, hi you two. I didn't see you there. I was just, just going to go inside. Fried chicken night! I, uh, geesh, I hope I have some chicken. I didn't, uh, didn't, well, I just lost my train of thought," said Ethan, giving them his best howdy-neighbor smile.

Reg spoke up. "You doing OK, buddy?"

"No, I'd say I'm not doing very good right now. Elise is gone."

Lonni gasped.

"She died today and I don't know what to do. I mean, I really want that fried chicken, I guess. Or I could sit here for awhile. What should I do?"

"Ethan, we are so sorry. Damn! She struggled and suffered so much. You should do what makes you comfortable. You want to sit in your car, sit in your car. We can keep an eye on you. You need some help with anything or have an errand for us to run, let us know. We're here for, OK?" said Reg.

"Thanks Reg. You and Lonni have been so good to us, even before Elise became ill. I'll never forget that. I think for now, I'll sit here a bit before I go inside. It's going to be difficult being in an empty house, knowing she will never be there again." Ethan hung his head.

"You want us to stay with you awhile?" asked Lonni.

"No. I'll be fine. I think I just need to be sad for awhile."

Plus, you two have some gardening to do. You guys have the nicest looking yard around. You should be proud of that."

"You're too kind," said Lonni.

"What's this fried chicken all about?" asked Reg.

Ethan meticulously sifted through his neat stack of papers, set in orderly piles on the dining room table. The aroma of chicken still filled the house. He licked his fingers. "Still not as good as yours, Elise. I tried," he said.

One more box lay at his feet. A shiny gray square about two feet wide, two feet long, and a foot tall. Sealed with clear tape and labeled, in Elise's handwriting, My Thoughts, Hopes, Dreams, and Wishes. She told him about the box and asked him to leave it sealed until she passed. Ethan glanced at the box, then at some hospital survey that greeted him with,

"The staff at St. Mark's Hospital hope your visit went well and you are now on the mend. Please take five minutes to... ." Though he laughed, he realized it was, to say the least, lacking in empathy. "Do you think everyone in your care comes out alive?" With disgust, he crumpled up the form and tossed it in the wastebasket at his side. The wastebasket sat next to that gray box.

That gray box.

"I see you. Don't think I'm not aware and I'll get to you soon. Please don't be like Pandora's box; I've had enough problems. Did you know that in Greek mythology, it was not a box but a jar? Yep, somebody mistranslated and now it's Pandora's box. Flash forward to today and I'm talking to a fucking box!"

Ethan walked around the table and placed the stacks in file folders. Those folders then went into one of two banker boxes. From there, he moved the boxes to his office and left them next to his filing cabinets.

Back at the table, he paused and considered that box. "Thoughts, hopes, dreams, and wishes. This feels like this will be a tough day. For you, love, I'll do it."

With that, he sat down, placing the box in front of him. There it was, perhaps the last form of communication with Elise he would ever have. He froze at the thought. His fingers tapped out a melody on the box, Fur Elise. He often played the opening melody without thinking; how many times did he tap that out on her arm, shoulder, or back? Hundreds? Thousands? It always made her smile. This time was one time he was quite aware of his actions. After he played the tune, he held the box up in the air, turning it to get a view of all sides, the top, and the bottom. She had sealed the box well. Ethan reached into his pocket for his folding knife, opened up the blade, and placed it over one edge of the top. Taking a deep breath, he methodically sliced the tape along the sides and then on top, down the middle. This cut also sliced through her label.

He paused again after setting the knife on the table. He was at once eager to see what treasure she left and terrified by the same thought.

"Quit staring at it Ethan and open it! Deep breath, exhale ... slowly. Deep breath, exhale ... slowly."

He grasped the two sections of box top, treating it as one would handle a bomb, with professional deliberation, taking care to not disturb the mysterious contents just behind the cardboard. As the box opened up, he recognized her writing, neat and confident. ETHAN was all it said on the envelope. He held the envelope to his nose, hoping for her scent, but there was none. Turning the envelope over and over, he imagined what it would say. "Surely its nothing bad," he said. "My god, we always talked out our problems or differences. There's no reason to think the worst. Get it together man!"

He quickly tore open the envelope, unfolded the letter, and began to read.

"My Ethan. If you are reading this, it means that I am no longer with you. An accident, a disease, or, hopefully very old age has taken me from you. It has ended us. I'm moved to tears just writing this, praying the day is decades away."

Ethan wiped away his tears and continued reading.

"We were blessed, having had so much time together, so much love and joy. You were always there for me and I hope you feel the same way about me. If I have any regret, it's that we did not have that family we dreamed about. Yes, we tried (and that was fun too!) but it was not meant to be. Aside from that, I leave this world regret free and full of our love.

"Now to the main reasons for this letter and the few items in the box. We had our conversations about the afterlife, religion, and what we both believe. Of course, my beliefs pretty well aligned with yours so there should be no surprises here. I just have a few requests that I hope you can honor. If this finds you 105 years old, blind, and in a wheelchair, then stay home, for everyone's safety!"

"I love your sense of humor!" said Ethan.

"If you are able, I ask this of you; I wish for my cremains to be scattered in the Pacific Ocean, off the coast of Oregon in that special town we visited so often; you know the one."

"Yachats. Of course." He stood up and walked into the living room. There, on the wall next to the front door, was a photo of the pair. They were holding hands on the beach with waves crashing behind them. This was the coastline at Yachats, Oregon.

Book Excerpt - The Knowledge Boy

I often sit amongst the reeds of brown and dying grass. They clatter against one another; their soft music fueled by a strong but inconsistent breeze. I come here to calm my mind; to slow down the procession of thoughts, ideas, images, and lesson plans. Those lesson plans! You see, my life has been all about teaching; more succinctly, transferring knowledge to citizens in the government's attempt at keeping Artificial Intelligence in its place. My mind is full of those lessons; interrupting my thoughts; commercials woven within the movie that is my life. I've been training New Thought Citizen Couples for generations now. Those couples were my adoptive parents until the day they died. A mourning period of one week was usually given. I would then be assigned to new parents and begin the knowledge transfer all over. I was twelve when I met my first parents. I was twelve when they died years later. I've been twelve ever since I turned twelve. However, that is just my physical age, frozen in time. Mentally, I am a Sage, destined to be hundreds of years older, churning through the lesson plans until...until when I do not know. Those plans are live, pulsing images in my cerebellum. Recollection is a simple task, usually instantaneous, often without awareness — as if I were breathing knowledge. Physics, basic and advanced; there they are. Look here, it's Beginner's Calculus sidled up against a class called History of Interplanetary Exploration — this class reflects on everything from Galileo's discoveries to the daring first Martian landing and is one of my favorites. Further along in my memory, and for no obvious reason, Animal Husbandry cozies up next to Theology and the Rise of Martin Luther. They're all there, thousands of plans, and I've presented them all dozens of times to hundreds of people.

I'm also here practicing my disappearance. Mine, and the departure of other SyOms, who, like me, wish to change phases. In case you are not aware, the term SyOms is derived from our scholarly title, scienta omnis, meaning 'all knowledge' in Latin. Our lives, extended past the tolerations of the individuals, have become a daily torture. Our controllers do not feel this way; the expectation is to train the population for an indeterminate time frame; it may be hundreds of years before our usefulness ends. Living with so many sets of parents is engaging at first. They are eager and willing to learn. They are the top minds in their fields. They also know that I will always be twelve and tend to accept that. I can't. I want to grow up, grow old and live out my life to its natural conclusion. If you've lost your parents, perhaps you can recall the pain and sorrow of their passing causes. Imagine doing that dozens of times. I mourn them all, especially when my mind is still.

Since I do not yet know my final outcome, I will provide you with every-thing I know about our society; where it came from, where it went, and what I hope it becomes.

And since you are hearing or reading this recording and have access to the embedded documents, my diary is no longer a secret. I have either been terminated by the Office of Tactical Teams Operations (OTTO); make no mistake, they are a government police force, my attempted DNA reversal failed with catastrophic results, or, and I dreamed of this for decades, the DNA reversal succeeded and I have died an old man. The first two scenarios guarantee no one will ever know about me. No one except for executive-level OTTO personnel, and, naturally, Secretary Helena Idalina Cole-Gilchrist and her inner circle of associates; said associates might not include her superior, President Hamza Izan Cole.

Cole-Gilchrist rose to the cabinet-level position of Secretary of the Home-land Intelligentsia Collective (HIC) in 2057, fourteen years after her phase reversal. She is the most powerful person on the planet. Yes, she was once a SyOms. Just like me.

I am Hugo Iker Cole, S.O.

My first assignment was with the Carletons, Raymond and Cynthia. Before my arrival, they received the letter of notice. An older couple, both tenured professors of mathematics at a private university. I provided them with my advanced mathematics knowledge and stayed with them until they were both institutionalized because of advanced dementia. Medical science would lead you to believe the aging process could be stopped — not slowed — and brain functions magnified to levels never imagined. Yet, treatment protocols for dementia had changed little since 1995. Their passing planted a seed of distrust and made keeping this journal, and its utmost secrecy, essential.

But I'm getting ahead of myself. I must, and as is logical, begin at the beginning. I'm speaking not just about my origin, but about how our country changed itself in order to protect itself. Its geography, politics, and social constructs changed rapidly.

The early 21st century found America, then known as the United States of America and comprising only fifty states, in the early technological stages of artificial intelligence (AI). The world debated AIs use and ramifications; not always peacefully.

Fears that false information would be rampant grew rapidly and not without merit. Businesses considered AI and the bottom line, with many embracing the technology. Politicos considered its use; legitimate, public-enriching projects and the hidden-from-view, self-serving diversions. Writers were questioned at every turn. Has any of your work been generated by AI? Those who denied using it but later found to be frauds were ostracized in the literary community. Often the government would stifle those authors — unless it served their agenda. Rarely would the industry monitored itself. Once AI companies started getting the algorithms more accurate, the more difficult it became to discover those machine-made works. Multiple tyrannical governments developed the technology at a quickened pace. The advancements would then be used to subvert their own citizens, that is, those not aligned with the government's ideals, and citizens of their enemies.

This would be the most prudent section to provide you with some historical perspective — of myself and the department I have been associated with for seemingly endless years.

I was born in the year 2030 to parents whose names are still classified, as are all parents enlisted for the fledgling program.

Book Excerpt - Three Bullets

May 19, 1977, Thursday night, 9:14

Two explosions tore through the night air. The shock waves left the vehicle's occupants' ears ringing. The man felt such pain, more intense than any he'd ever experienced as it gripped his upper body. His breath faltered. He gasped for air, smelling the powerful odor of burnt gunpowder. His left arm was now a numb, lifeless appendage. Strange, other-worldly, and muffled sounds ebbed and flowed around him, breath-like and pulsing.

He trembled, a dread enveloping his entire being, far more profound than mere fear. He sensed the darkness behind him. This pang grabbed his soul and crushed his spirit. He shuddered, sensing the end rushing his way.

His eyes opened; two narrow slits. Everything was blurry as his eyelids fluttered open and closed multiple times, trying to focus. Regaining a sense of clarity was a struggle. The right side of his balding head, with close-cropped graying hair along the sides, bounced off the passenger window. A fuzzy glow from the orange-tinted sodium street lights flickered and faded across the dashboard. The lights washed across his face as the car rolled down the freeway; destination, unknown. His ears rang with a confusing mix of sounds. The tires created a steady hum, and an occasional clap-clump, clap-clump as the tires slapped the pavement when they traveled over a bridge. He heard two men yelling at each other.

Blood trickled down the white leather interior. It soaked the doorsill as it descended; it flowed down to the crack in the door. There, the wind caught the red gore, fanning it out along the side of the automobile.

His eyes widened. His body tensed as he ignored the pain. Who's blood is that? My god, is that mine? It is! What is happening to me? Why am I here? And just where is here?

Those thoughts raced through his mind, one on top of another. The pain in his shoulder was relentless, and the man wondered if he'd ever catch his breath. An odd, wet-sounding wheeze rattled with every exhale. The fear surged forward again. Heart pounding, the memories flooded back.

Two strangers, one stood just outside the garage door as he pulled up to the townhouse complex. One man brandished a gun, tapping it against his thigh. The other man, quite diminutive in stature, snuck up behind him. He made a slow, sweeping motion with his hand, and without speaking a word, he ordered him to pull the Cadillac forward, out of the light, and into his garage. Once out of public view, both men raised their arms. He stopped his car.

He snapped back to the present. That crushing dread surrounded him again. He shifted his attention as he thought of his daughter, wishing to be near her again. How to get out of this mess? He tried to shift to the left, but the agony in his shoulder and the sticky, metallic taste of blood in his mouth made him stop. Weakness overpowered him, and the fear screamed at him. His thoughts drifted in and out of focus.

Sounding as if underwater, a muffled voice said, " ... like a mob hit. It'll throw the cops off the trail." That's not possible. Did he understand that correctly? He wanted to tell them, let them know they were mistaken. He was no mobster. Why did they say this? It just made no sense. Maybe he misheard. His mind and heart raced at a frantic pace.

The two strangers yelled at each other again, but the muffled words rendered them unintelligible. It reminded the man of times that, as a very young boy, he would rest in his mother's arms, drifting off to sleep. He could almost hear her talking to other adults as they sat around the kitchen table, voices deep, soft, and comforting. Despite all the agony, a smile crossed his face. Inner peace chased the terror.

The yelling continued, and the peace he felt evaporated. As he shifted his focus to the present, he knew he had to make a move, and he had to do it now.

Make eye contact with them and talk to them, he told himself, believing words could get him out of this trouble. He'd always been an excellent negotiator. Tell them he would get them money, they could have his car, his watch, whatever they wanted.

Could he escape this nightmare? He turned his head towards the driver. Through half-opened eyes, he saw the gun barrel and felt the weapon's hard steel end as it pressed against his temple. His bloodshot eyes bulged wide with fear. He tilted his body to the right, pushing his head into the soft padding of the passenger door. The gun barrel followed him, pressed firm and uncomfortable against his bare skin. What else was there to say? How could he save himself? His mouth opened to speak.

In an instant, a bright flash of light filled the interior of the car. He never heard another sound; never uttered another word.

Anthony Warren Werner never thought of anything else ever again.

Eleven days earlier ...

May 8, 1977, Sunday morning, 6:30

A moment of sorrow caught Anthony Werner off guard as he dried and stacked the few dishes he used for breakfast. It had been a decade since his wife had died of cancer and he often mourned her. Kathy was his true love. These simple moments in life gave him pause. Melancholy would wash over him. Sadness would grab at him, as it regularly happened while doing those unremarkable chores; vacuuming, dusting, or cleaning a window. He knew he had to visit her whenever this heartache would burn.

He would gaze towards the sky and talk to her. "What fun is it, having all these nice things, these beautiful trinkets and objects when you are not here? There is our daughter, she has enjoyed them. It's not the same without you, Kathy. And don't even give me any guff concerning my dating life. It occupies my time. Doing something with someone, nothing more. Without you, trips to the market, movies, restaurants, and all of life's joys are torture. It's as simple as that. I wish you had never left us, that the doctors could have helped more. And I can hear you now, 'Tony, don't mope. And don't be so sad!' See you soon, Kathy."

He dried off his hands, grabbed his keys, and crossed the parking lot to his garage. Anthony breathed in the cool dawn air and unlocked the side door of his garage. A thin film of dust danced in the early morning sunlight that burned through the windows as he climbed into his car. As a lifelong Cadillac owner, this 1977 Coupe de Ville caught his eye on the dealer's lot. The white exterior with a white interior was something he'd not seen before, and he loved it. The dealer mentioned that the man who ordered the fine automobile filed for bankruptcy. That stopped the deal in its tracks. Tony bought the car the first day he saw it, three short weeks ago.

Before leaving, he popped the trunk open and made sure he had his cleaning supplies he kept in a small box. "This trip will do me good," he said as he shut the trunk.

Kathy's gravesite was a thirty-minute drive out in the country near the farm where she was raised. The dark green fields of grain, rolling hills, and stretches of flatland were beautiful, peaceful, and timeless.

"Oh, I love how tranquil it is out here," he once said to her.

"Me too. What a wonderful space to spend eternity together," whispered her voice in his memory as the cityscape turned to farmland.

Anthony felt the fresh country air the second he stepped out of his car and onto the cemetery grounds. "Let's get your stone tidied up. What do you say, Kathy?" he asked as he reached for the box inside the trunk.

He kneeled next to their shared headstone, crossed himself, and hung his head in silence for several minutes. Small tears formed in the corners of his eyes. He read the lettering etched in the stone, as he'd done countless times. 'Katharine Louise Werner 1918-1967' and next to that, 'Anthony Warren Werner 1916-'. His eyes stopped at the blank space after his year of birth and he wondered when the engraver would carve the numbers. What would it say?

"Alright, Tony, snap out of it. Let's get after it! Hmm, looks like a country crow left you a present, Kathy. Gosh, those crows always scared you." He didn't hide his laughter. "Sorry for laughing, dear, but I can remember the time there was a mother bird that would not leave you alone. You spent half the summer walking across the yard instead of the sidewalk to avoid that bird and her nest! Oh, how you would scream!" He took a deep breath and sprayed water on the stone with an extra squirt for the bird's business. His hands made slow, sweeping circles, swirling a damp rag across the granite face. A sad smile crossed his face as he pictured her last days of suffering. When he was done, the stone was shining, and he had clipped the grass along the edges, as expert as any gardener. He was careful to scoop up the cut blades and disperse them in the gravel drive next to his vehicle. He walked back to collect his box of supplies, kissed the palm of his hand, and placed it against her name.

"You've been gone for ten years. I just can't believe that. Sometimes I'm afraid I might not remember the sound of your voice. I would rather die than forget anything about you. Until next time, my love."

Anthony always enjoyed the drive back into the city. It allowed him a chance to reflect. Behind his car, a slow-motion rooster tail of gravel dust gave way to the muted sound of tires on the blacktop. The countryside changed to cityscape. His mind shifted from the past to the present. He was always aware of this transformation. It never failed to refresh his soul.

Once back in town, he stopped off at the gas station to have his tank refilled.

"Mr. Werner. Great to see you!" said the attendant.

"Hi Tommy. Just fill it up, please. I'll get a car wash later. Need to get back home in a hurry."

"You got it."

With the car fueled up, Anthony took a side trip to the home of his daughter, Kaylie. He often dropped by unannounced, and she was always glad to see him.

"There's my little girl," he said to himself, "getting her flower bed ready." He pulled into her driveway and rolled down the passenger window. "Hey, you! Prepping your plants for summer, are you?"

"Daddy!" She pulled herself up, brushed the dirt off of her jeans, and ran over to the open window. "Hi! What a surprise. What are you doing out this beautiful morning?"

"I was out visiting your mom's grave and heading home."

"Oh, Daddy, how nice! I'm going to place some flowers there soon. Does everything look OK out there today?"

"Yes, fine, fine. Everything there is looking good. I just did some cleanup."

"Hey, your eyes look a little red. Are you OK?"

"Yes, the visit made me sad today, realizing that it's been ten years since … well."

"I know. Would you like to come in? Adam was planning on stopping over around noon for lunch. Please join us."

"Thanks, but I'm going to head home, maybe stay away from work today. I just wanted to see you and to tell you I love you."

She ran around the back of his car and pulled his door open. "I love you very much!" she said as she planted a kiss on his forehead. "Not working tonight, you say? I don't believe that for an instant!"

"I don't believe it either," he winked at her, "but I am going to go home. Call me later this week."

"I will call you soon. Love you, Daddy."

"Love you too, little girl."

Anthony pulled out of her drive and was back in his townhouse fifteen minutes later. Hunkered down at the desk in his home office, he laughed, "You know me too well, Kaylie." He opened his briefcase and started reviewing his next project, another home remodel.

The phone rang, breaking his concentration. He picked up the receiver. "Hello, this is Anthony."

"Hi Dad! It's Kaylie. I wanted to make sure you're OK. I've been thinking about her a lot, too."

"I'm doing fine, honest."

"You're working right now, aren't you?"

He let out a deep-from-the-gut belly laugh.

"I knew it! I just knew it. Daddy, go to bed early."

"Yes ma'am. We'll talk soon, Kaylie."

"Bye-bye, Daddy." And after he hung up, she added, "I'd do anything for that man!"

May 8, 1977, Sunday morning, 11:52

Dale Bowers was dead broke and looking to make some cash. He had no problem getting money any way he could, legal or not. Having no steady income was typical for Dale. Convicted felons with bad tempers make prospective employers look elsewhere.

The interior of the convenience store was bustling with customers paying for gas, making their way to the self-serve coffee machine, or just hanging out to pass the time. He was about to have a chance encounter that would be a life changer, and not just his.

Dale pushed the door open with the middle of his back and stepped out into the midday air. He held an unopened pack of cigarettes in one hand and an overcooked, greasy hot dog in the other. As the door shut behind him, a rusty, oil-burning Volkswagen clanked and clamored into the parking lot.

"Hey you old son of a bitch!" the man yelled and cackled through the open front passenger window.

Dale, somewhat startled, shot his eyes toward the voice, his body tensing. His fight instinct subsided once he recognized the man.

These two men first met three years earlier in, what never seemed to them to be an odd meeting place, the county jail. He had spent the night in lockup on a drunk and disorderly charge after getting into a fight in a bar. His new friend was finishing up a six-month stint for burglary.

"Well, shit! How the hell are ya, Big Man?" said Dale as he opened the passenger door, uninvited.

Dale slapped the man on his shoulder and he flopped down on the front passenger seat as if he owned the place. He took several bites of the hot dog, smacking his lips with each bite.

"Again with the 'Big Man'? You know I hate that name, dude."

"Gordo, don't be so sensitive, man. I only call you that, so I don't confuse you with all the other Gordons I know. There's a lot of guys named Gordon in this world!"

"Bullshit, even I don't know any other guys named Gordon!"

"Plus, I just like busting your balls when I see you. Damn, good to see you."

The old cellmate, Gordon Thompson, had the ironic street name, 'Big Man', because of his short stature. The running joke among his felonious friends was that he was five foot-one when he had blisters on his feet and weighed almost 110 pounds soaking wet with a full stomach. Everyone who knew him would laugh at his nickname, but he despised the moniker. Out of desperation, he dealt with it — he had to belong somewhere.

"What have you been up to, Dale? Staying out of lockup, I hope."

"Yeah, mostly, I've avoided county. I've been looking to earn some money," he said, pulling an empty jean pocket inside out.

"It's tough out there. I have a buddy in construction. Want a construction job?"

"No, I do not. They wouldn't want me either, if they checked my record."

"What are you wanting to do?"

"Nobody is going to want to hire this old convict. Doesn't leave me with too many choices."

"So, jobs that are less than legit? Got it." Gordon was someone who kept his eyes open for opportunities, both for himself and his friends, legal or otherwise. "Well, I know a guy who might have something for you. I've been trying to keep my nose clean, so I try to avoid him. Now, he mentioned this one side job the other day."

"Who've you been talking to and what's the job?"

"This guy's name is Steve. Does construction — same guy who might know of construction jobs — but he talked about a guy he knows that would be easy to roll. Like I said, I'm trying to avoid that line of work. I didn't pay much attention to details."

"Can you talk to him? Maybe set up a meeting between him and me? I'm about out of money, man."

"Let me try to talk to this guy and I'll get something set up. How do I get back to ya?"

"Meet me down the street at that car lot," he said, pointing over Big Man's right shoulder, "tonight at five o'clock. If anybody gets nosy, we're just looking at the used cars. Bring this piece of shit to make that story believable."

Big Man laughed, but Dale stared him down with a deadly serious look.

"Five will work. I have to meet my parole officer at three thirty," said Big Man, holding up an official-looking letter. "But don't worry, I'll be there. It's just that, damn, you're kind of rushing me on this."

"I'm kinda fucking broke, so I need this, OK? I suppose you need a cut, too."

"Damn, take it easy Dale, take it easy. I don't want nothing, alright? Not a fucking thing, man. Consider it a favor as old cell mates, OK? Maybe down the line something big comes up. Keep me in mind."

Dale let out a long, slow exhale and climbed out of the car.

"Listen, man, I'll get the scoop on this for you tonight. Promise. And I don't want a cut, really." Big Man smiled at Dale as he stuffed the letter in his back pocket. By now, he just wanted to get out of there as soon as he could. He was already sorry he stopped at that convenience store.

"Yeah, don't be late," said Dale, slapping his hand on the roof of the car. And as he walked away from Big Man, he said, out of earshot, "Bullshit, everyone wants something."

Big Man, forgetting why he stopped at the store, drove away. His car still making noises and puffing smoke. "Just do him this favor and walk away Gordon, easy money is too tempting," he said, feeling sick to his stomach.

After walking off to the side of the store and up a small hill, Dale sat himself on the ground against a large maple tree. He had nowhere to go and no one else to see the rest of the day. He'd just wait until 5:00 p.m. and walk over to the car lot. The steady hum of traffic and the wind rustling the leaves above his head relaxed him.

"Ah, this is the life," he said. Even he didn't believe that as he drifted off to sleep.

Dale woke up with the sun in his eyes, the big maple tree no longer shading him. "Shit! What time is it?" he asked, but he was alone. He looked at his left wrist but only saw the pale outline of a watch he used to own, having pawned it five days earlier. The pawn shop owner gave him eight bucks for the watch, out of pity. It only provided enough for a couple of small meals and the hot dog and pack of cigarettes he had today. Dale ran down the hill to the convenience store. A young woman with short blonde hair was getting out of a silver Datsun. "Excuse me, pretty lady. Can you tell me what time it is?" he asked her.

She stopped, looked at him from head to toe, and shook her head. "No, I don't have my watch with me."

She entered the store as Dale kept asking people for the time. "That guy bugs me," she said to the cashier. "I don't like his looks."

"That guy is bad news. Stay away from that one," replied the cashier.

"Four forty-five, young man," said a passing customer.

"Thank you sir," said Dale, "you made my day." Dale turned and walked down the street to the car lot. He leaned against a concrete pillar that held the large signpost of the dealer. The sign's sharp red and blue letters on a field of white plastic proclaimed, 'Wheeler Motors — Buy and Sell — Wheel 'er In Or Wheel 'er Out'.

Dale opened up his new pack of cigarettes and lit one up, slowly exhaling the smoke.

"Hey buddy, we can't have you loitering. You need to move along," said a man dressed in slacks, a short-sleeve shirt, and a very short tie.

"Yeah, well, I'm a customer. More like a buddy of mine is. He should pull in soon, driving an old smoking shit box. I told him I'd meet him here and I'd help find a new car. My friend doesn't know cars very well."

"My mistake. Do you know what your friend is looking for or how much he wants to spend?"

"No, I don't. I figured him and I could just walk around by ourselves first and then come in and deal."

"Sure, if you want to do that. We're open until seven," said the salesman. He headed back inside, but kept a close eye on Dale.

At precisely five o'clock, Big Man pulled into the lot and parked behind a row of used cars.

Dale walked up to the driver's side window. "Well, give me some good news."

"Steve will meet you tomorrow. He figured he'll get off work around five-thirty so you two can talk then. There's a guy he has in mind. Same guy as I mentioned to you earlier."

"So where do I meet him?"

"He's doing construction on the west side. He'll be on a new road called, get this, Peaceful Valley Lane. Who names these streets anyway? To get to this new street, go three or four blocks west of 56th Street off of Lincoln. Do you have a car or need a ride?"

"I have a car, just conserving the gas. I'll handle it from here. Thanks buddy, I owe you one."

"Forget it Dale," said Big Man, "you know I got your back."

Dale spied the car dealer stepping outside, and he was heading their way. "Crap, let's get out of here. That guy thinks you're going to buy a car."

"I can't afford a car, Dale!" said Big Man as he fired up his car. Dale climbed in the front. Chugging and smoking, they rolled off down the street and out of sight.

"Yeah, your buddy's going to buy a car. Bullshit, he didn't even get out. You bum!" yelled the car dealer.

About The Author

Born in Des Moines, Iowa, Jeff spent his formative years chasing bugs, playing sports and riding his bike around the neighborhood. Once forced to grow up, he spent 42 years in the information technology field, before retiring in 2022.

His retirement freed up time to pursue writing, an avocation that has always interested him. He is currently working on an encyclopedia of minor league baseball in Des Moines, a new detective series, a work of dystopian fiction, and whatever else should pop into his mind.

When not busy writing, he also enjoys bringing new life to old pieces of furniture, target shooting, spending time with his German Shepherd Dogs, Jax, and Jaycie, and living the life with the love of his life, Constance.